Draw

Perspective

DAVID BROWN

Series editors: David a

A & C Black • London

First published 1982
New style of paperback binding 1996
by A&C Black (Publishers)
37 Soho Square
London W1D 3QZ

Reprinted 1999, 2001, 2002

ISBN 0-7136-6246-8

Printed in Hong Kong by Wing King Tong

Cover photograph by Zul Mukhida

Contents

Making a start   4

What to draw with   6

Proportion   10

Composition   12

In general   13 .

Linear perspective and 'eye level'   14

Linear perspective:
   frontal   15
   worm's-eye   16
   bird's-eye   17

More about vanishing points   18

Step by step:
   frontal   22
   worm's eye   24
   bird's eye   26

Reflections   28

Difficult subjects   30

Circles and ellipses   38

Foreshortening   40

An awkward combination   44

Tonal or aerial perspective   45

Line and tone combined   46

Line and tone compared   48

Making a start

Learning to draw is largely a matter of practice and observation — so draw as much and as often as you can, and use your eyes all the time. The less you think about how you are drawing and the more you think about *what* you are drawing, the better your drawing will be.

The best equipment will not itself make you a better artist — a masterpiece can be drawn with a stump of pencil on a scrap of paper. But good equipment is encouraging and pleasant to use, so buy the best you can can afford and don't be afraid to use it freely.

Experiment with the biggest piece of paper and the boldest, softest piece of chalk or crayon you can find, filling the paper with lines to get a feeling of freedom. Even if you think you have a gift for tiny delicate line drawings with a fine pen or pencil, this is worth trying. It will act as a 'loosening up' exercise. The results may surprise you.

Be self-critical. If a drawing looks wrong, scrap it and start again. A second, third or even fourth attempt will often be better than the first, because you are learning more about the subject all the time. Use an eraser as little as possible — piecemeal correction won't help. Don't re-trace your lines. If a line is right the first time, leave it alone — heavier re-drawing leads to a dull, mechanical look.

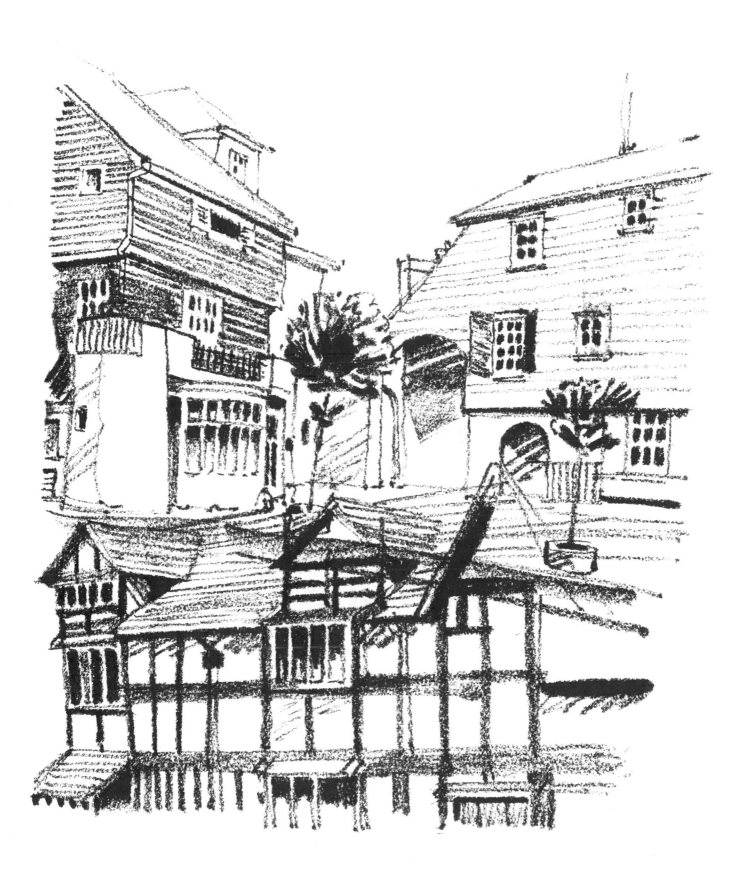

What to draw with

Pencils are graded according to hardness, from 6H (the hardest) through 5H, 4H, 3H, 2H to H; then HB; then B, through 2B, 3B, 4B, 5B up to 6B (the softest). For most purposes, a soft pencil (HB or softer) is best. If you keep it sharp, it will draw as fine a line as a hard pencil but with less pressure, which makes it easier to control. Sometimes it is effective to smudge the line with your finger or an eraser, but if you do this too much the drawing will look woolly. A fine range of graphite drawing pencils is Royal Sovereign.

Charcoal (which is very soft) is excellent for large, bold sketches, but not for detail. If you use it, beware of accidental smudging. A drawing can even be dusted or rubbed off the paper altogether. To prevent this, spray with fixative. Charcoal pencils, such as the Royal Sovereign, are also very useful.

Pastels (available in a wide range of colours) are softer still. Since drawings in pastel are usually called 'paintings', they are really beyond the scope of this book.

Pens vary as much as pencils or crayons. The Gillott 659 is a very popular crowquill pen. Ink has a quality of its own, but of course it cannot be erased. Mapping pens are only suitable for delicate detail and minute cross-hatching.

Special artist's pens, such as the Gillott 303, or the Gillott 404, allow you a more varied line according to the angle at which you hold them and the pressure you use.

Reed, bamboo and quill pens are good for bold lines and you can make the nib end narrower or wider with the help of a sharp knife or razor blade. This kind of pen has to be dipped frequently into the ink.

Inks also vary. Waterproof Indian ink quickly clogs the pen. Pelikan Fount India, which is nearly as black, flows more smoothly and does not leave a varnishy deposit on the pen. Ordinary fountain-pen or writing inks (black, blue, green or brown) are not so opaque and give a drawing more variety of tone. You can mix water with ink to make it thinner, but for Indian ink use distilled or rain water because ordinary water will make it curdle.

Ball point pens make a drawing look a bit mechanical, but they are cheap and fool-proof and useful for quick notes and scribbles.

Fibre pens are only slightly better, and their points wear down quickly.

Felt pens are useful for quick notes and sketches, but are not good for more elaborate and finished drawings.

Brushes are most versatile drawing instruments. The biggest sable brush has a fine point, and the smallest brush laid on its side provides a line broader than the broadest nib. You can add depth and variety to a pen or crayon drawing by washing over it with a brush dipped in clean water.

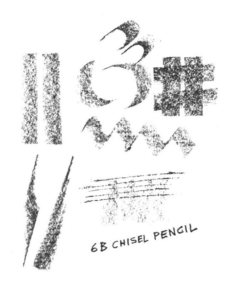

6B CHISEL PENCIL

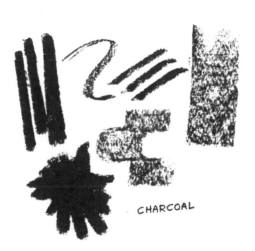

CHARCOAL

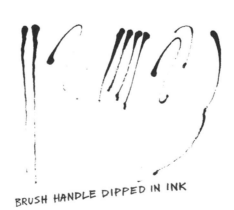

BRUSH HANDLE DIPPED IN INK

Mixed methods are often pleasing. Try making drawings with pen and pencil, pen and wax or wax crayon and wash. And try drawing with a pen on wet paper.

Experiment with various media. Discover their range and limitations. You will probably find that you prefer one to the others, so use it. If you don't enjoy your work, your enthusiasm will diminish. There's no point at this stage in struggling with a medium you don't like, but delay your decision until you have tried as many as possible. This does not mean that you should abandon all other media. When you have gained confidence with your chosen one, try the others again; you will be surprised what a little experience and confidence can do.

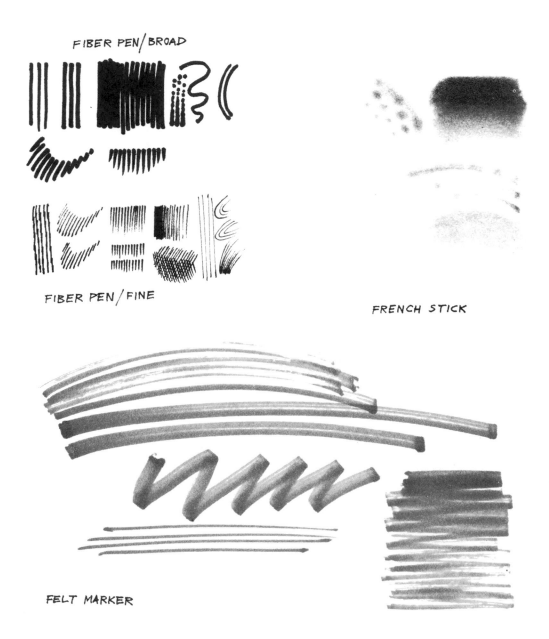

FIBER PEN/BROAD

FRENCH STICK

FIBER PEN/FINE

FELT MARKER

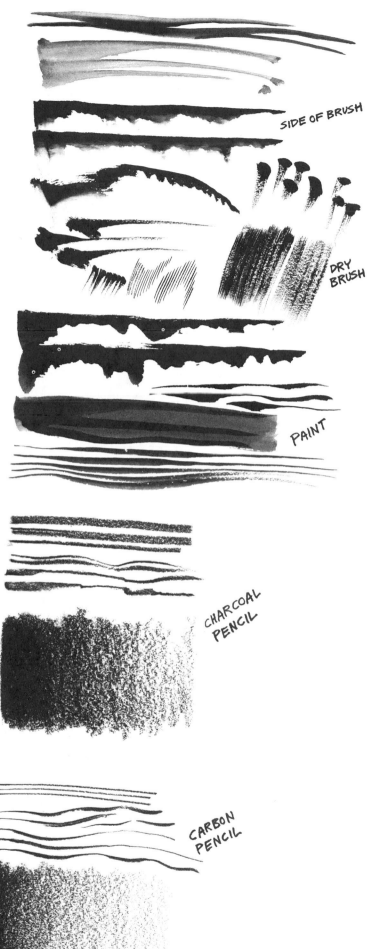

SIDE OF BRUSH

DRY BRUSH

PAINT

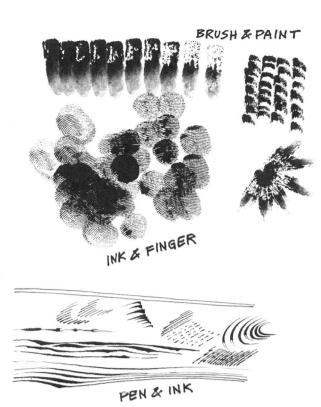

BRUSH & PAINT

INK & FINGER

PEN & INK

CHARCOAL PENCIL

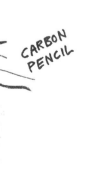

CARBON PENCIL

9

Proportion

The essence of good draughtsmanship is getting proportions right — which *must* be done when you are putting down your first basic lines.

A good way to make sure of this is to use one section of the subject you have chosen to draw as a unit of measure. For example, if you are drawing a building, use a window as your unit of measure.

Hold your pencil vertically at arm's length, with the top of the pencil in line with the top of the window; then place your thumb on the pencil to line up with the bottom of the window.

Use this measurement to work out how many windows make up the building's height, keeping your thumb on the same spot on the pencil and the pencil at arm's length.

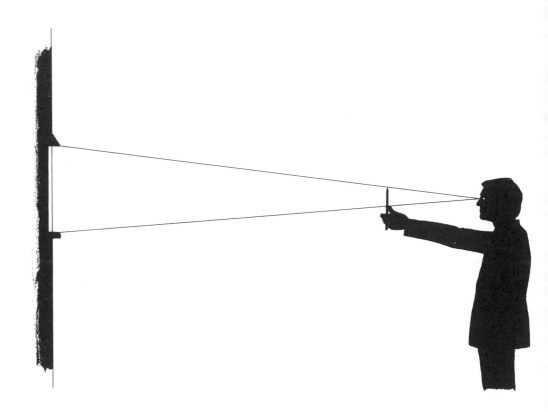

Now draw the window roughly and mark out the number of other windows you need to get the correct height and width of the building. You can now mark in the position of the various features of the building.

To make sure the roof sits correctly on the building, join up the corners of the side wall. Where the lines cross, draw a vertical line; this will give you the perspective centre of the building, above which the point of the roof should be.

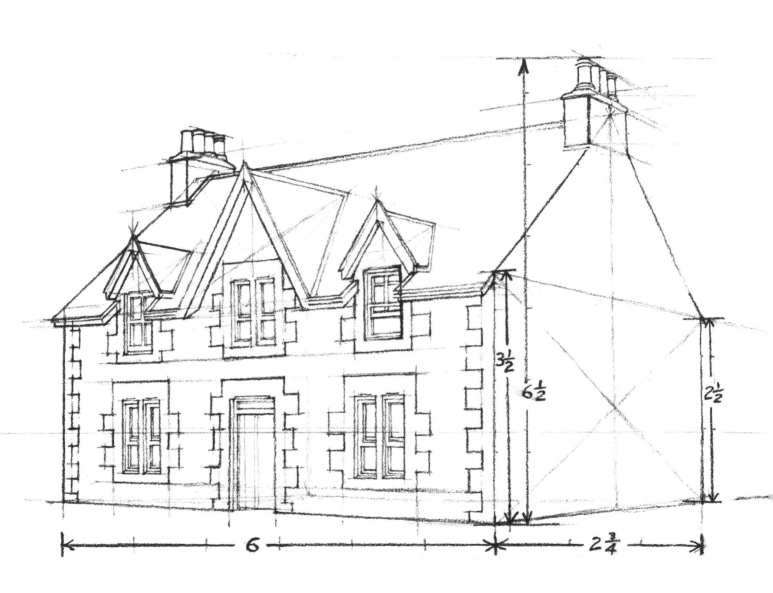

Composition

Deciding where to place even the smallest sketch or doodle on a scribbling pad involves composition. Any drawing is greatly affected by its position on the paper. Before you begin, therefore, think about how you will place your subject on the paper. Even a few seconds' thought may save your having to start all over again. Never distort your drawing in order to get it all in.

Cut out two pieces of card so that they form corners. Hold them up between you and your subject. Position them so that the inside edges of the card touch the outside edges of the subject (A). This will show you the proportion of the area taken up by the subject, and will help you to compose or position your drawing on the paper. In (B) the pieces of card are used as an adjustable picture frame, to help you decide how much of the subject you want to include.

Alternatively, draw in the middle of a large piece of paper, and cut the paper afterwards to make a composition that pleases you.

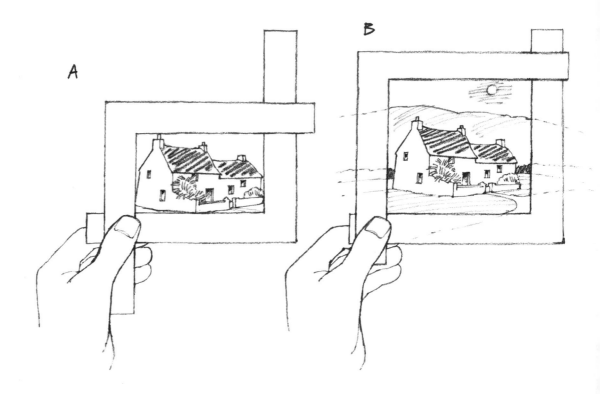

In general

Perspective in drawing is a method of conveying the appearance of distance and three dimensions on the flat, two-dimensional surface of paper, board, canvas, etc. One needs to understand that it is the expression of optical illusion. Two identical objects, one of them close to the observer and the other far away, appear to be different in size, whereas in reality their size is the same.

Either 'linear' or 'tonal' (also known as 'aerial') perspective can be used to convey this appearance of distance in a drawing. The choice between them depends on the nature of the subject. To get depth into a street scene, for example, it is normally better to use linear perspective; for a mountainous landscape, tonal perspective would probably be more suitable. It is easier for the beginning artist to learn about linear perspective first.

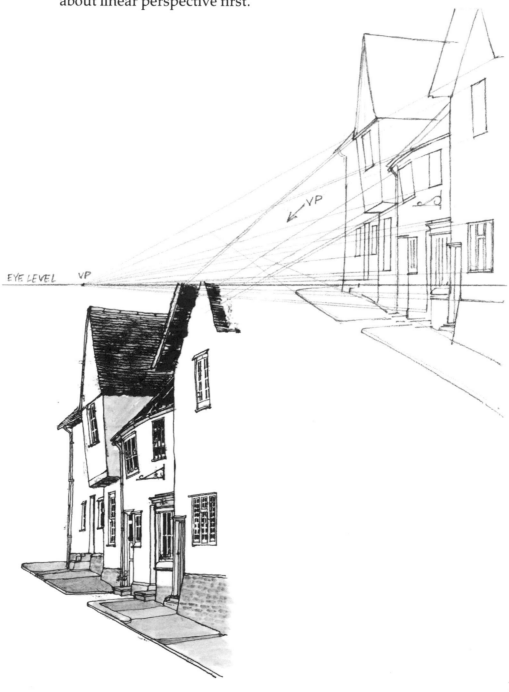

13

Linear perspective and 'eye level'

The expression, 'eye level' means exactly what it says: the level of your eyes above the ground, whether you are standing or sitting. All receding lines above your eye level run down to meet it, and all lines below rise to meet it; where they meet is known as 'the vanishing point'.

If you have difficulty in finding the position of your eye level (which can be a little confusing on sloping ground), draw some parallel lines onto a piece of glass: hold the glass at arm's length, positioning the centre line directly in front of and level with your eyes. The other parallel lines will help you to see more clearly the angles of the object you are looking at. Those above should slope down and those below should slope up.

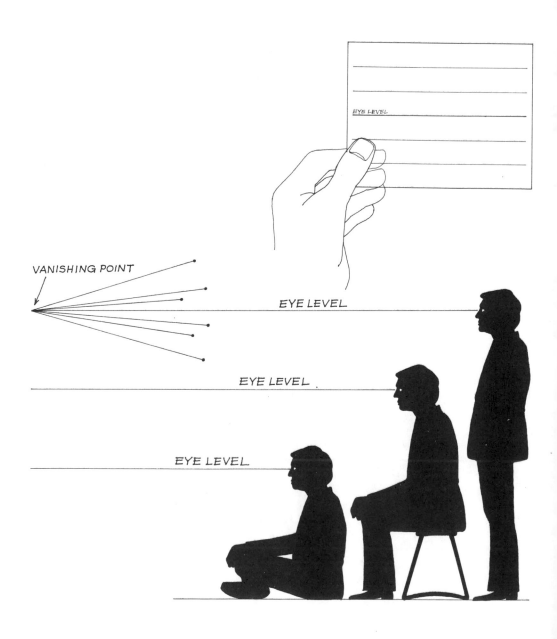

VANISHING POINT

EYE LEVEL

EYE LEVEL

EYE LEVEL

Linear perspective: frontal

The following three pages illustrate three basic eye-level positions: frontal (or normal viewing) as shown here, worm's-eye and bird's-eye views.

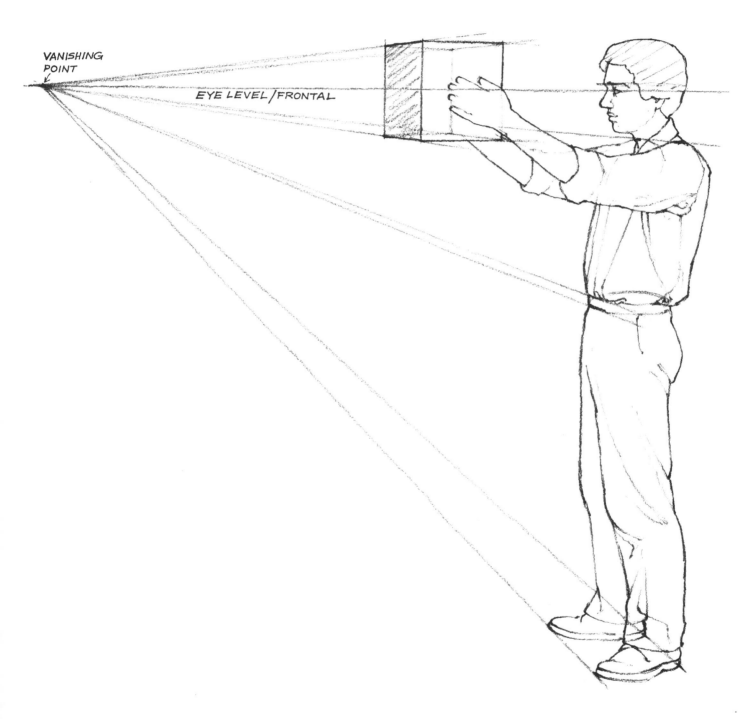

VANISHING
POINT

EYE LEVEL/FRONTAL

Linear perspective: worm's-eye

When you are squatting or lying down, your eye level is close to the ground, and your view is worm's-eye.

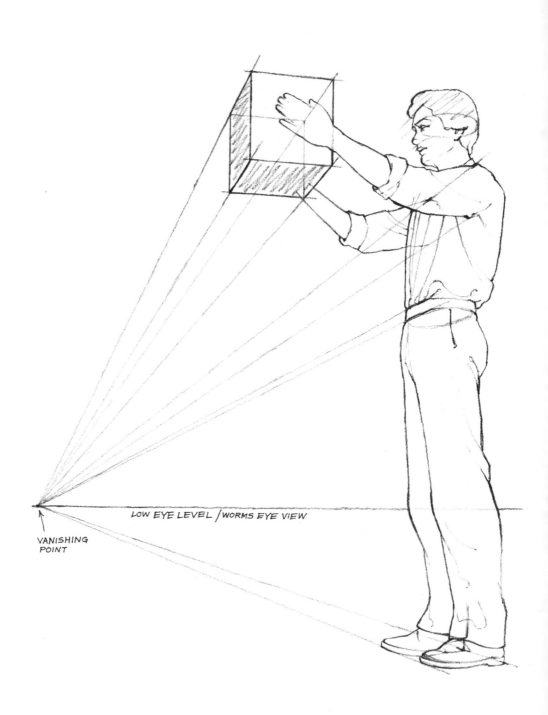

LOW EYE LEVEL / WORMS EYE VIEW

VANISHING
POINT

Linear perspective: bird's-eye

When you are above your subject — on a hill or looking out of an upstairs window — your eye level is high and your view is bird's-eye.

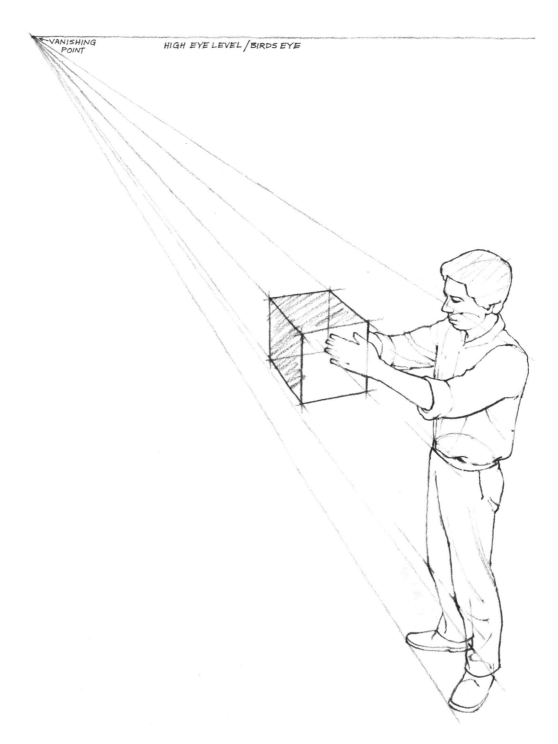

VANISHING POINT

HIGH EYE LEVEL / BIRDS EYE

More about vanishing points

In most drawings more than one vanishing point comes into play. Here, because the cubes are lying parallel to one another, there are only two.

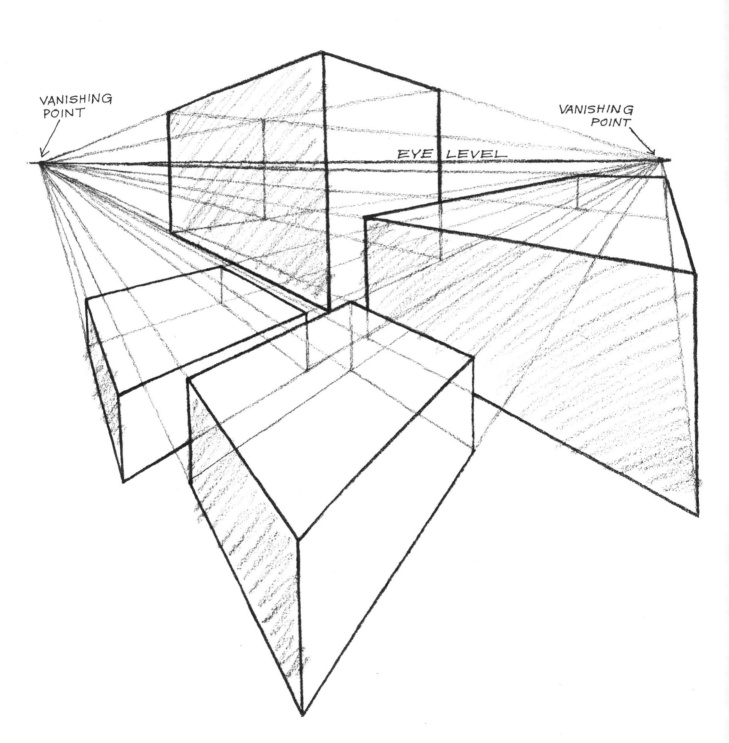

When objects are not lying parallel — as here — more vanishing points are needed.

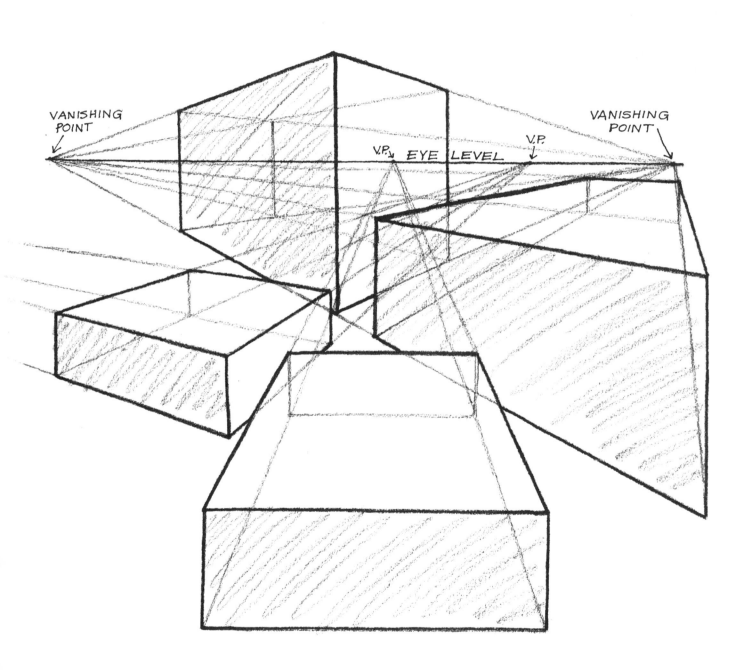

VANISHING POINT

V.P.

EYE LEVEL

V.P.

VANISHING POINT

Distance can be indicated without vanishing points — by reducing the areas between lines, as here.

If you combine this technique with that of lines vanishing to points on the eye level, as in the fibre pen sketches on the next page, you will convey a sense of distance very strongly.

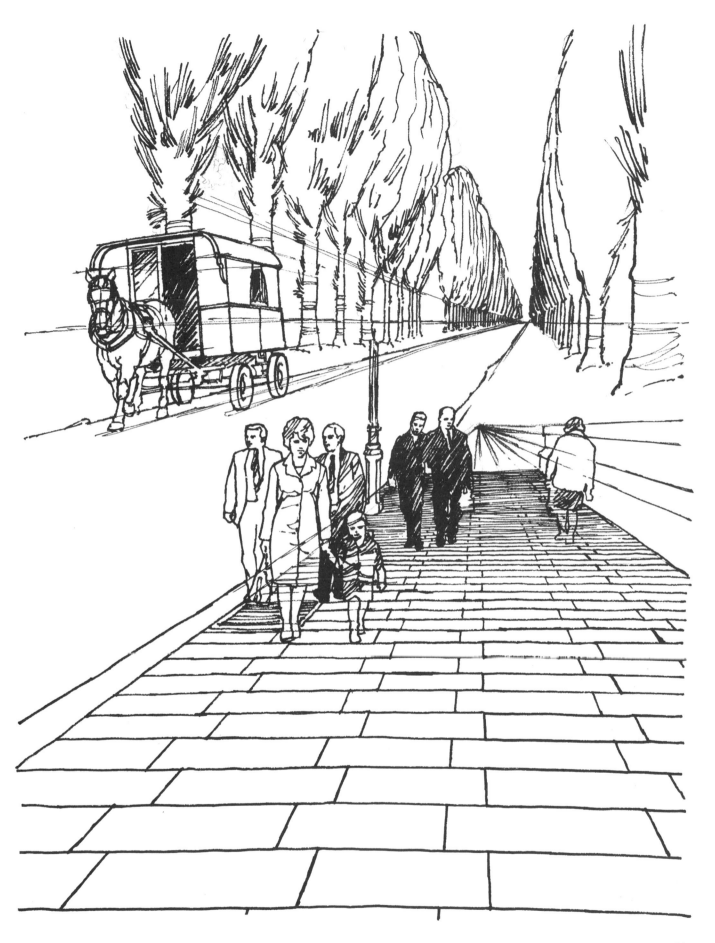

Step by step: frontal

First draw in your eye level.

Next, draw in the basic lines of your subject, making sure the proportions are correct. Details can be drawn in later. Notice the slope in the ground of the completed drawing here, and that I ignored this when sketching the base of the monument at the earlier stage above.

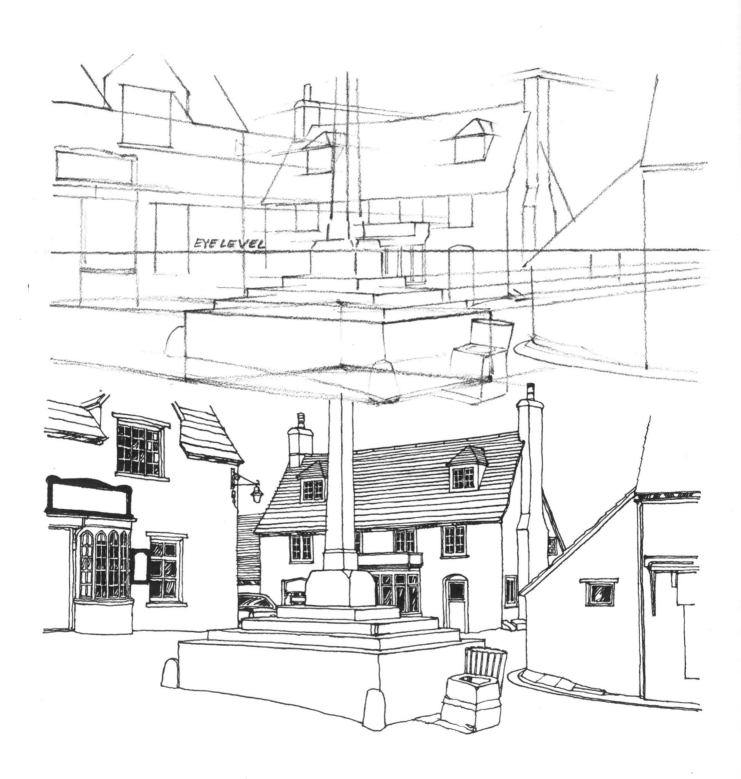

EYE LEVEL

When drawing in the basic shapes, draw roofs, etc., with straight lines. Characteristics of individual buildings, such as sagging roofs, can be added later.

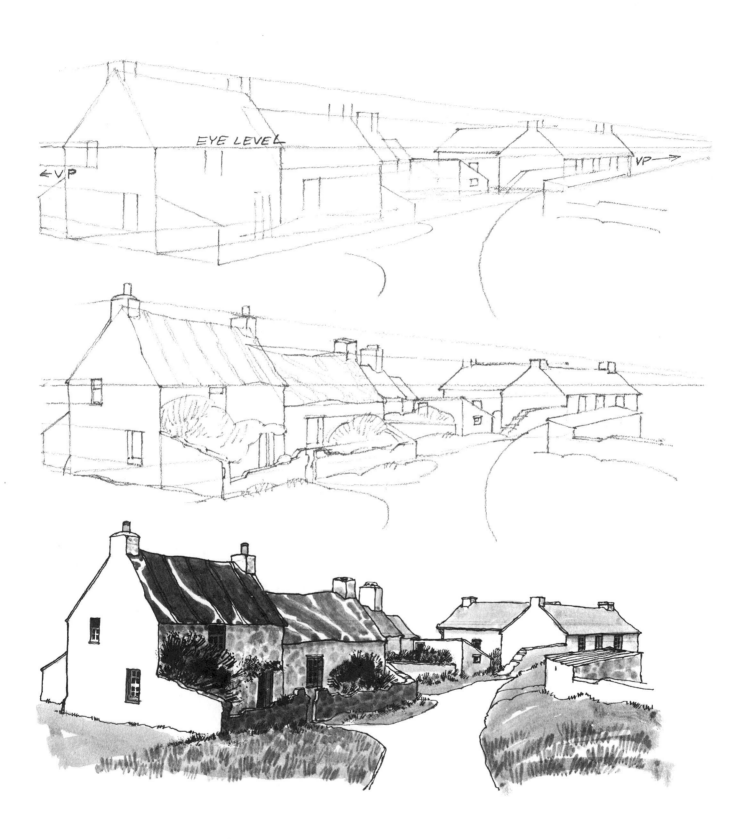

Step by step: worm's-eye

Here the ground slopes steeply, giving a worm's-eye view of the buildings. Notice that the steps change direction, which means a change of vanishing points.

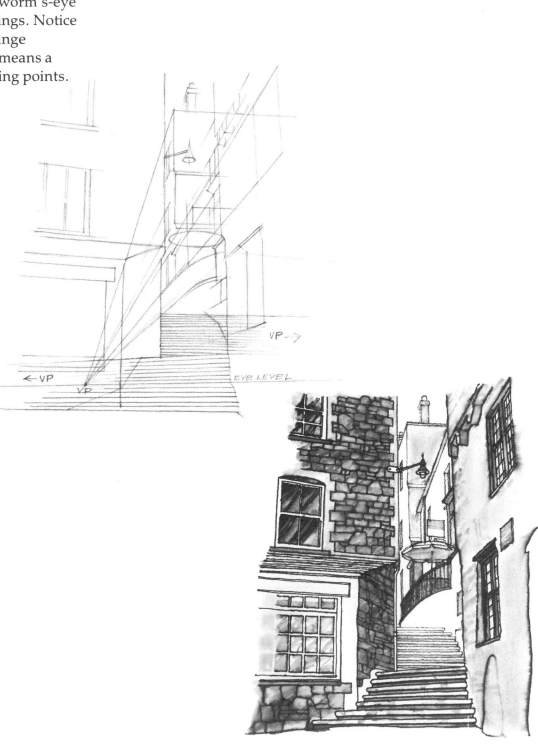

This worm's-eye view of
buildings and a cliff top is
seen from a beach. There are
several vanishing points
because the buildings,
arranged in a semi-circle,
present themselves at
different angles to the
viewer.

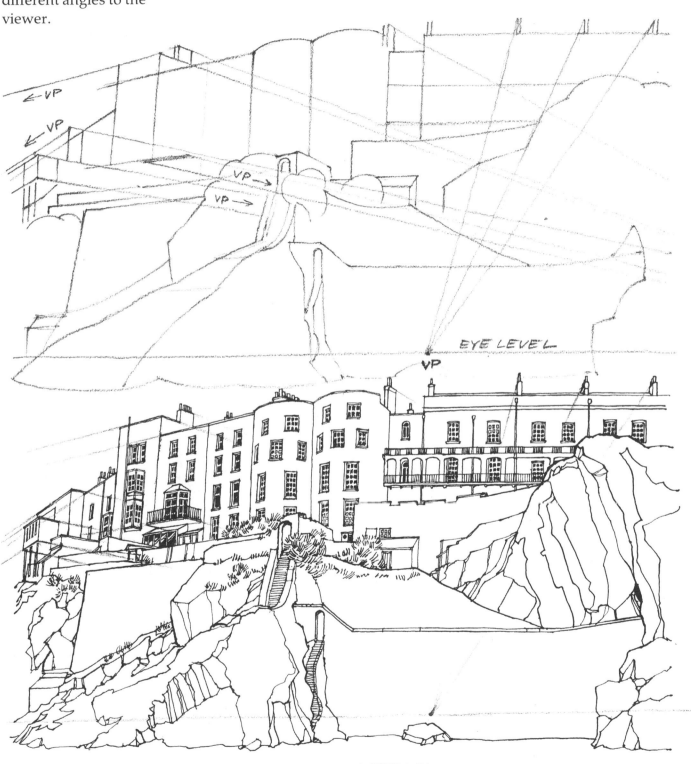

Step by step: bird's-eye

This is an unusual view from an interior balcony. The confined space produces dramatic angles and lines vanishing downwards as well as to the front and sides.

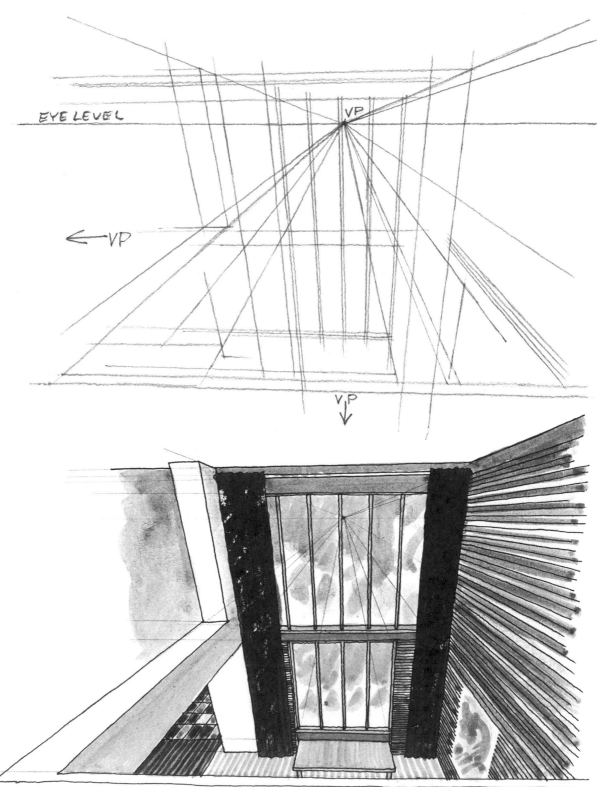

There is no difficulty here in sorting out the eye level — which is the horizon. Again, notice that the sloping beach at the base of the harbour wall is not suggested at the first, basic-line stage.

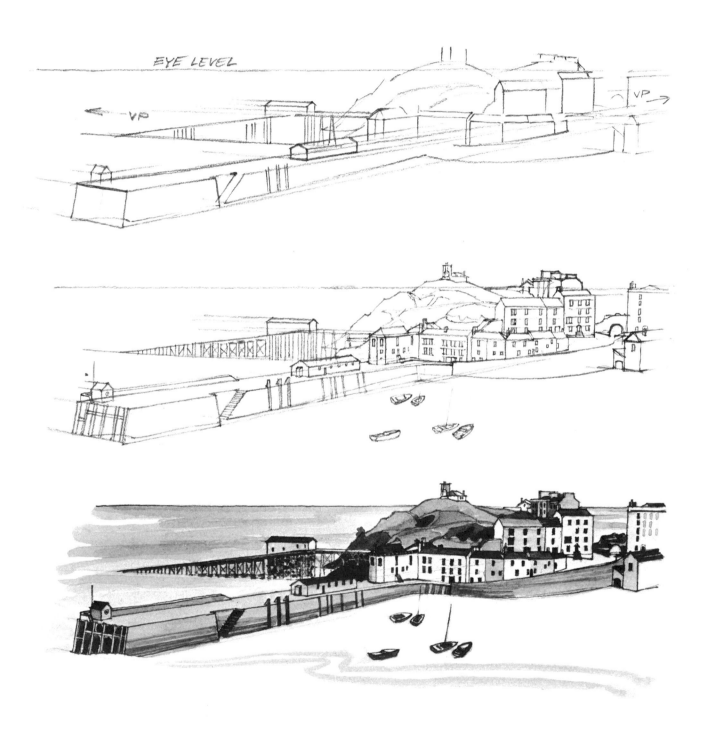

Reflections

Reflections will appear to be the same distance from a window or mirror as the object being reflected. This means they will appear in perspective, as shown in the diagram below.

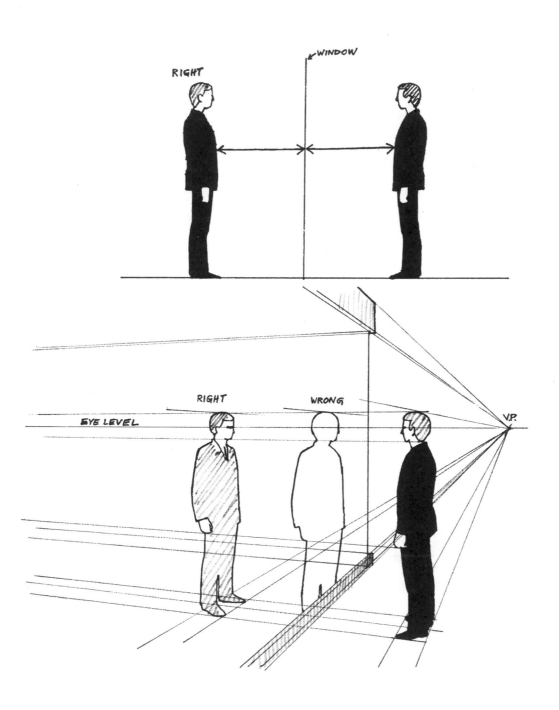

Study these sketches closely, turning the book upside down to compare the reflections with the objects being reflected. Notice, for example, how the position of the bridge changes in perspective in relation to that of the people; and that the reflection of the canopy supports on the boat vanishes to the same point as the original supports.

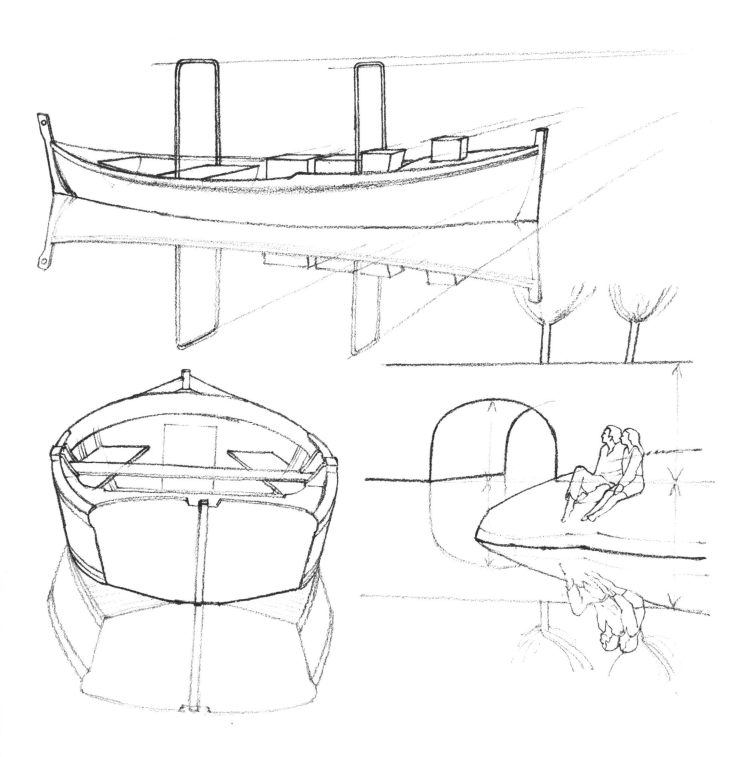

Difficult subjects

There are some subjects to which the laws of perspective are particularly difficult to apply. A boat is one. Diagram (A) below shows that there are several straight lines running across the boat which will enable you to use a vanishing point. But for the length of the boat there will normally be only one straight line (down the centre). The sides and seats have subtle curves and angles.

Look hard for anything you can use to help you get proportion and perspective right, such as seat supports, or any rectangular shape in the boat. In the top drawing here, I picked out the corner spots where the cabin joins the deck as fixed points from which I could achieve the perspective of the cabin's curved roof.

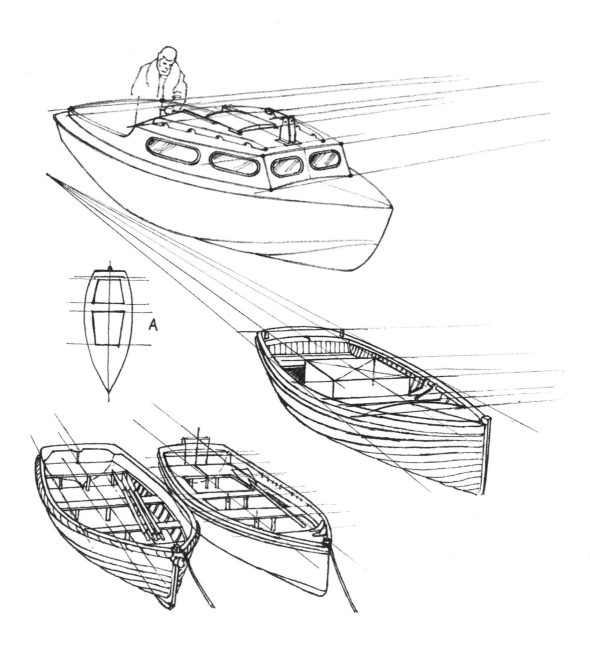

To help you understand what perspective does to the shape of a boat, draw the shape itself inside a rectangle on a piece of card. Tilt the card at different angles and study how the volume and shape of the areas change. For example, notice in diagram (B) that the half of the boat nearer to you occupies more space than the half further away.

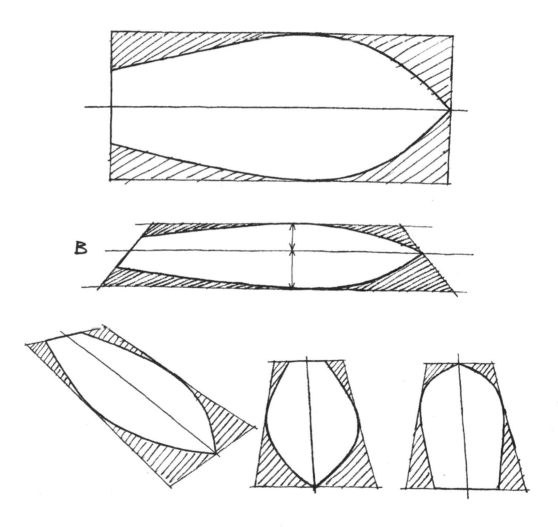

Like boats, sports cars need to be looked at carefully and various corresponding points lined up in order to establish vanishing points.

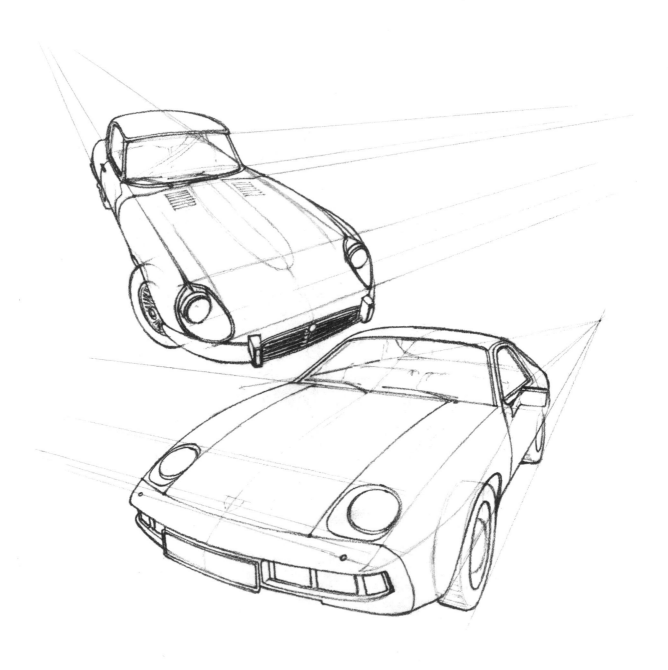

Angular vehicles, such as those illustrated here, are much easier to draw.

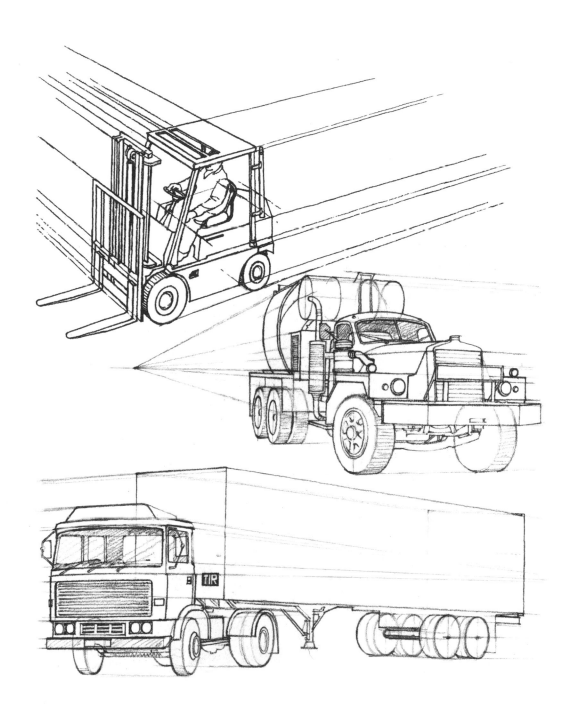

Old buildings can be difficult too. The upper floor on one of those depicted here has gradually settled into a forward position over the centuries, and one side is lower than the other. This puts it on a different plane to the rest of the building, with a different vanishing point. To complicate things further, all the buildings are on a hill.

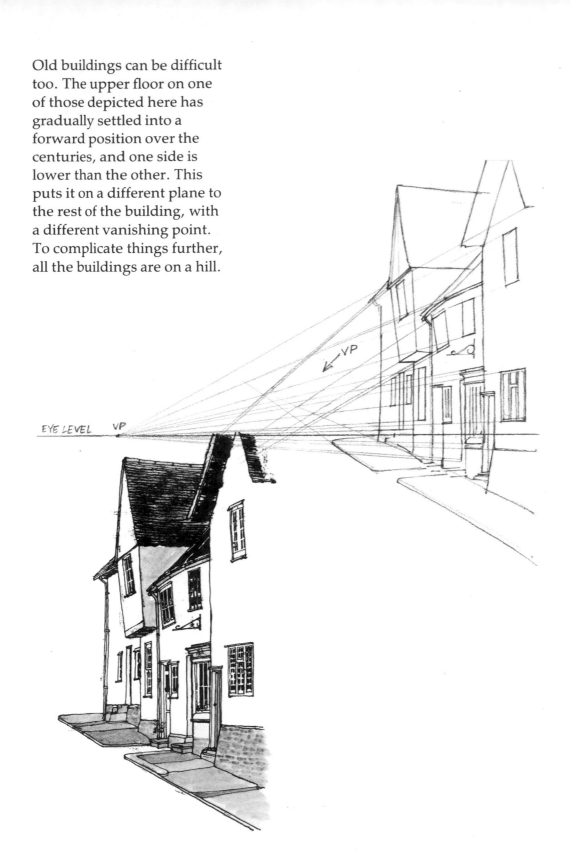

With a plant it is easier to
achieve perspective if you
start by drawing the basic
shape in its simplest form.

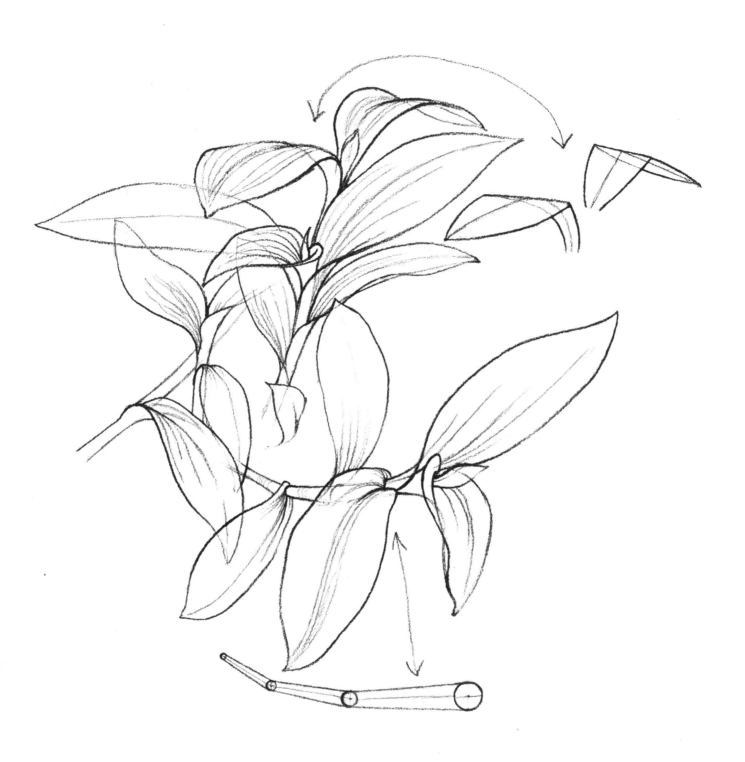

Interiors can be straightforward when the furniture is angular and arranged as this is.

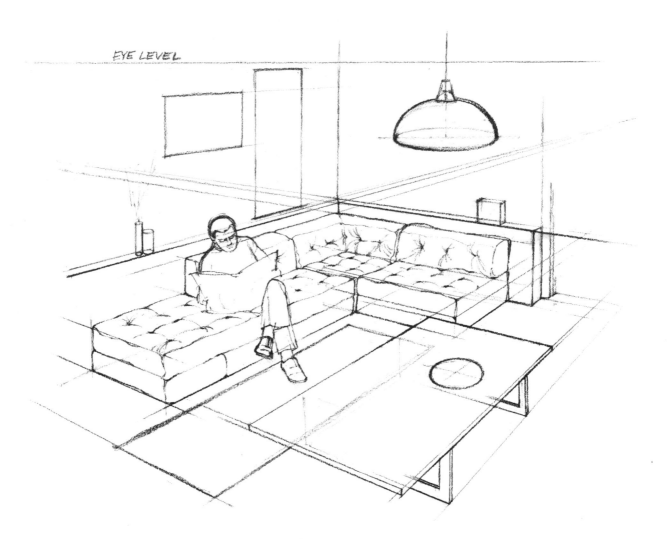

EYE LEVEL

Here, the situation is more complicated. Study the drawing on page 19. Because the furniture is arranged at different angles, each has its own vanishing point. Try to complete the objects by drawing the hidden parts, as illustrated below.

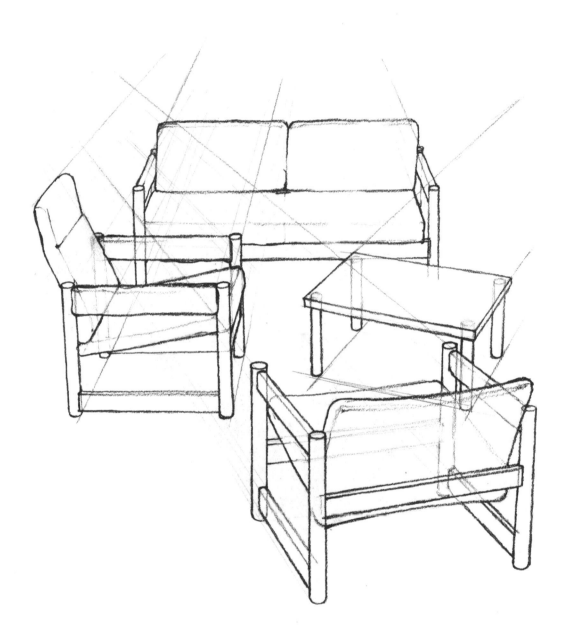

Circles and ellipses

Circular objects can be difficult because a circle becomes an ellipse when viewed at an angle. This diagram illustrates what happens. Never draw an ellipse with pointed ends (A).

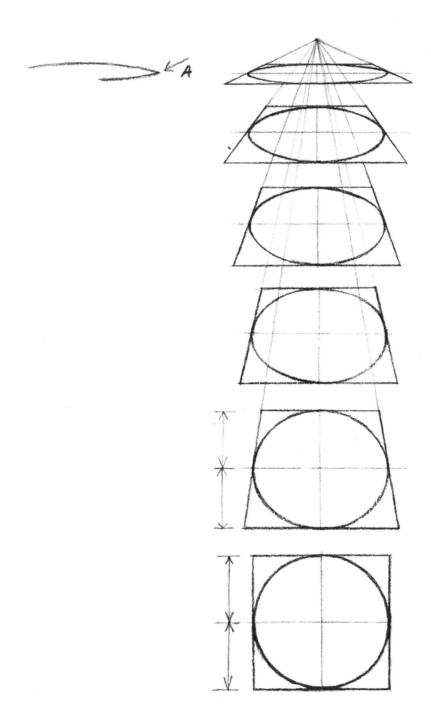

When drawing an ellipse,
first sketch in the centre line
and any other lines which
will help you to get the
shape right.

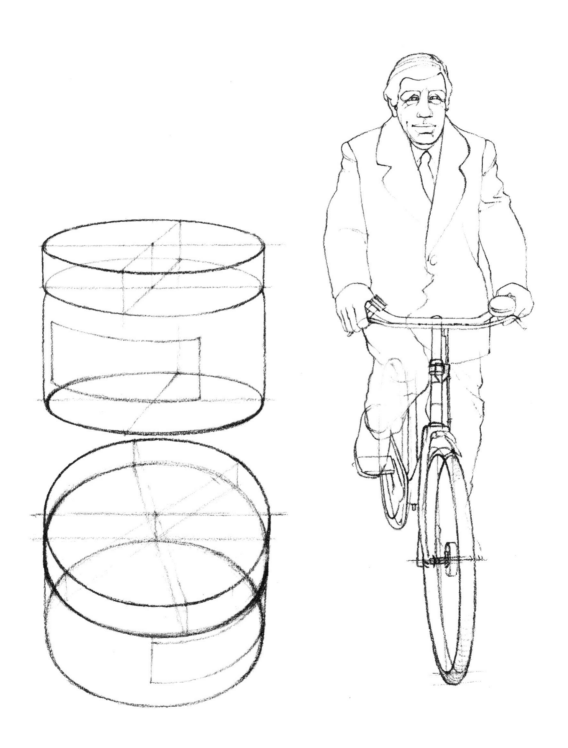

Foreshortening

Foreshortened views are more deceptive than you might think, and it is important when drawing a foreshortened view of an object to use carefully the unit-of-measurement method described on page 10. You will be surprised at the small area taken up by parts of your subject which, when seen face-on, are large. I used the distance from the tip of the nose to the chest as a unit of measure when drawing this sunbather.

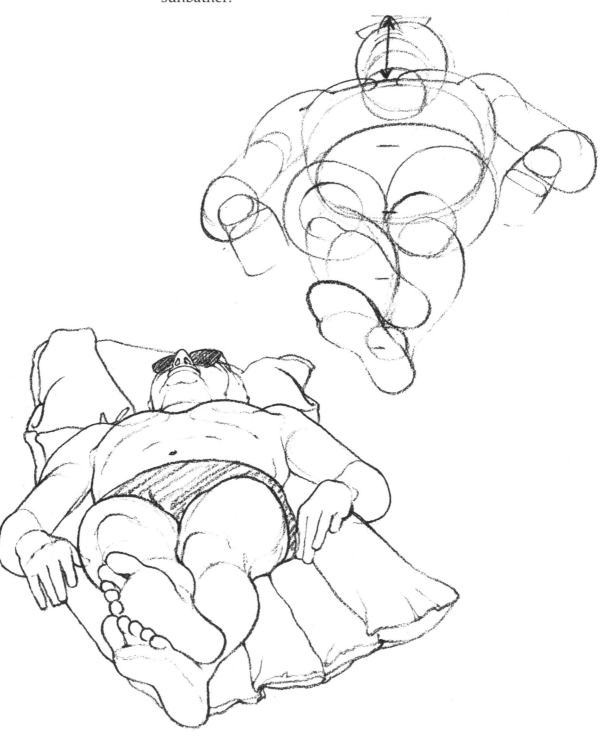

To practise foreshortening, seek the help of a friend or member of the family and make studies from different angles.

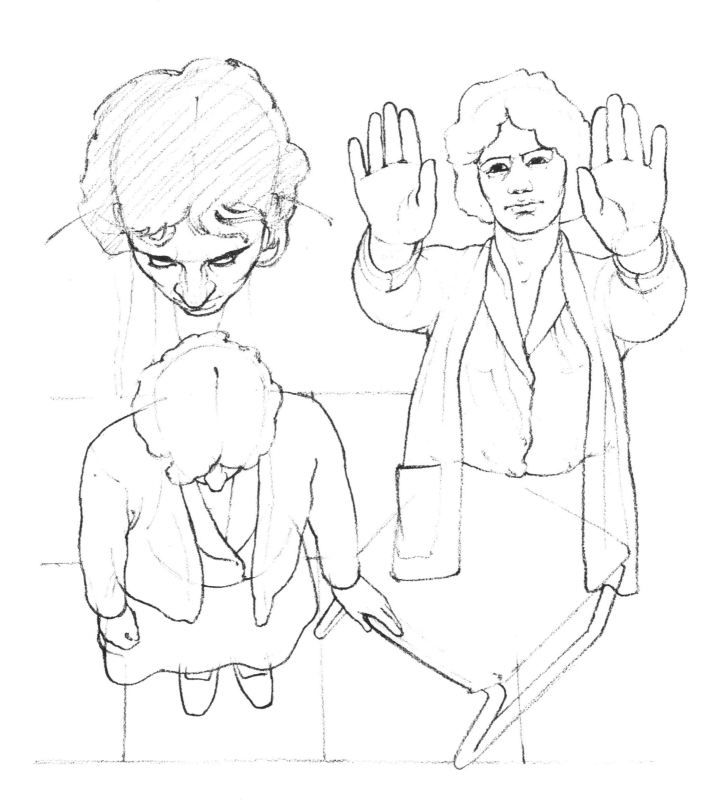

Notice on this page the area taken up by the front (A) of the foreshortened businessman's jet in comparison with that of the side (B).

The diagrams underneath illustrate the effect of foreshortening. The equal areas of the side view (C) are greatly reduced in the foreshortened drawing above, but the same details still need to be shown.

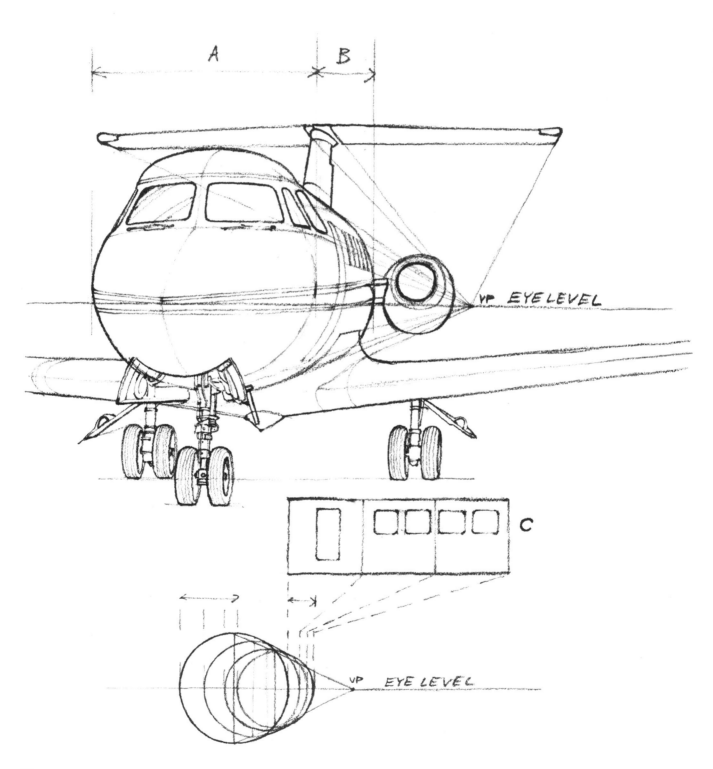

This page illustrates a simple method of conveying the foreshortened perspective of a bending road. On a separate piece of paper, rule parallel lines to form equal squares; then draw a bending road on it. Next, turn the top away from you and look along the paper to see what happens to the road. You can even bend the paper to simulate a hill or depression in the ground.

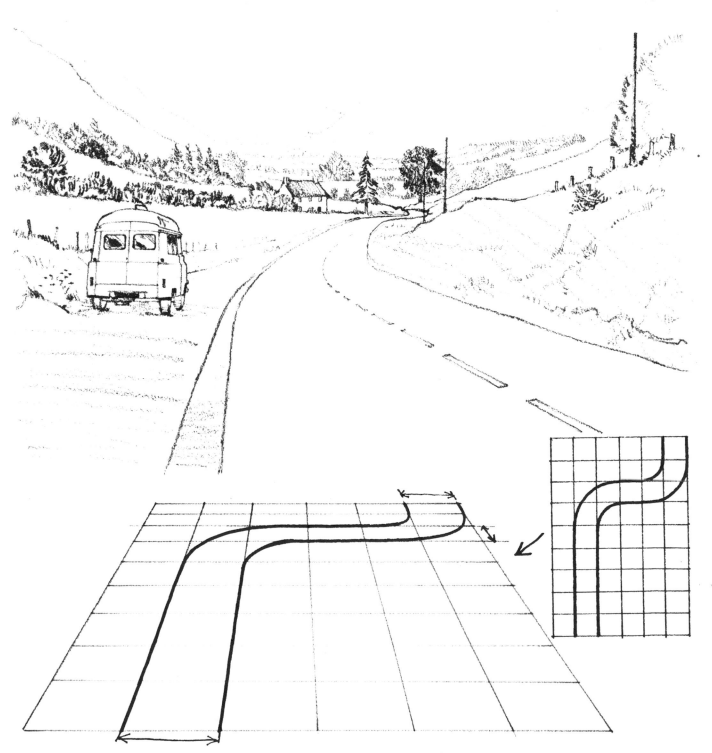

An awkward combination

In a scene containing a hill, buildings climbing up it will vanish to one point and the hill (which is on a different plane) to another. Movable objects on the hill, such as cars, will vanish to the same point as the hill.

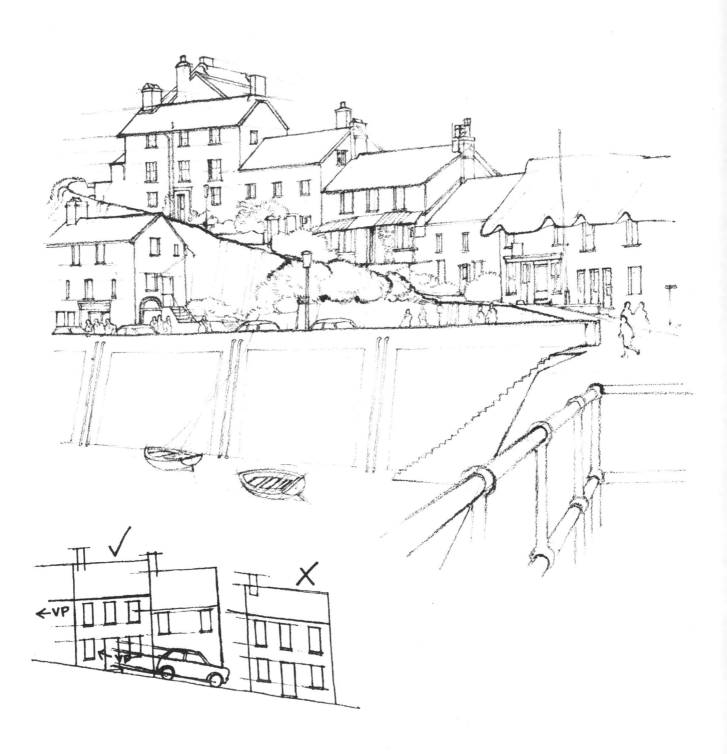

Tonal or aerial perspective

Where linear perspective is not possible or desirable, distance can be shown by varying the strength of tone in your drawing. Usually it is best to progress from darker, sharper tones in the foreground to lighter, softer tones in the background. You can practise tonal perspective simply by using different shades of grey felt pens when sketching. Leave out details to start with: concentrate on broad tones.

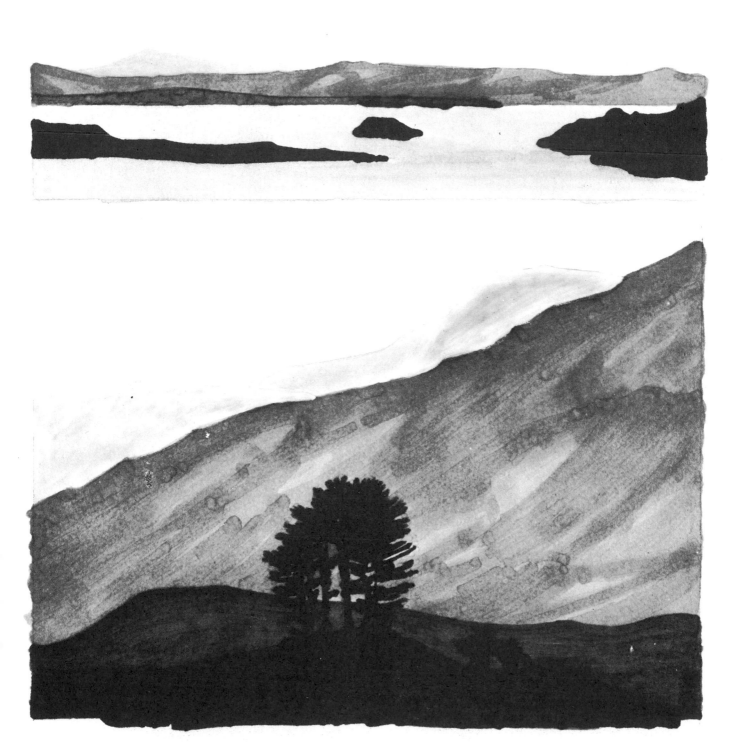

Line and tone combined

In a landscape containing some buildings, you may want to combine linear and tonal perspective, as in the finished drawing opposite. The eye level here was drawn for me: it is the horizon. Remember, when starting a picture like this, to simplify the shapes, concentrating on the basic lines.

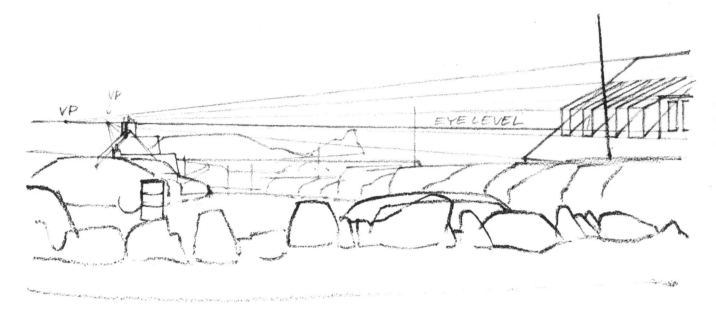

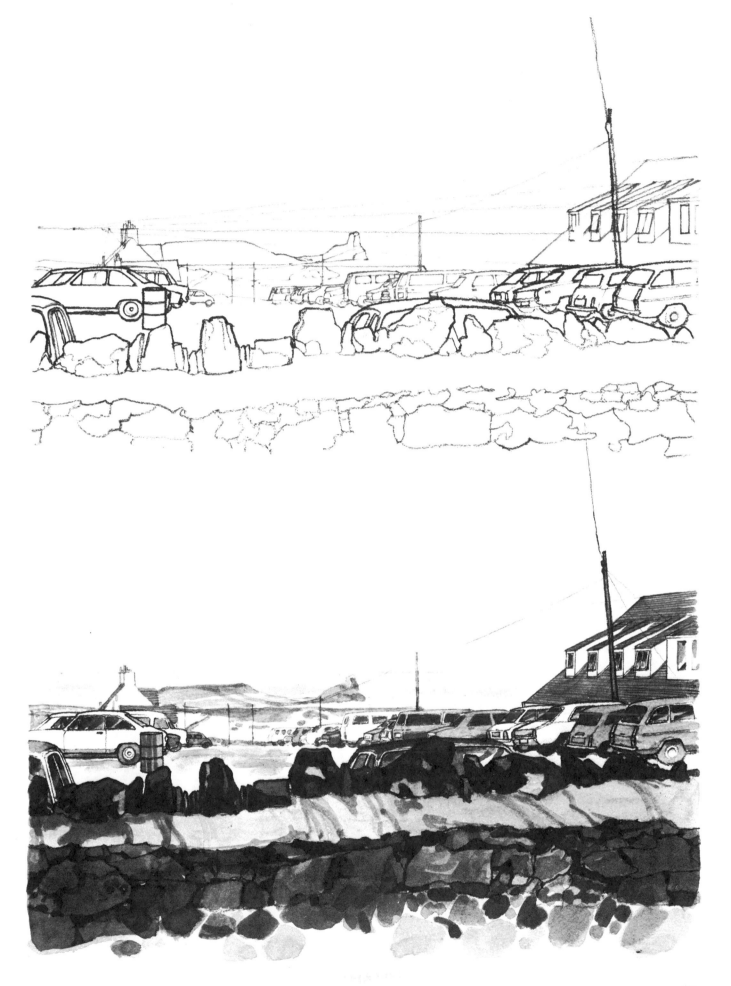

Line and tone compared

In the drawing on the left depth is conveyed by variations in the strength of line; in the drawing on the right by variations in both line and tone.

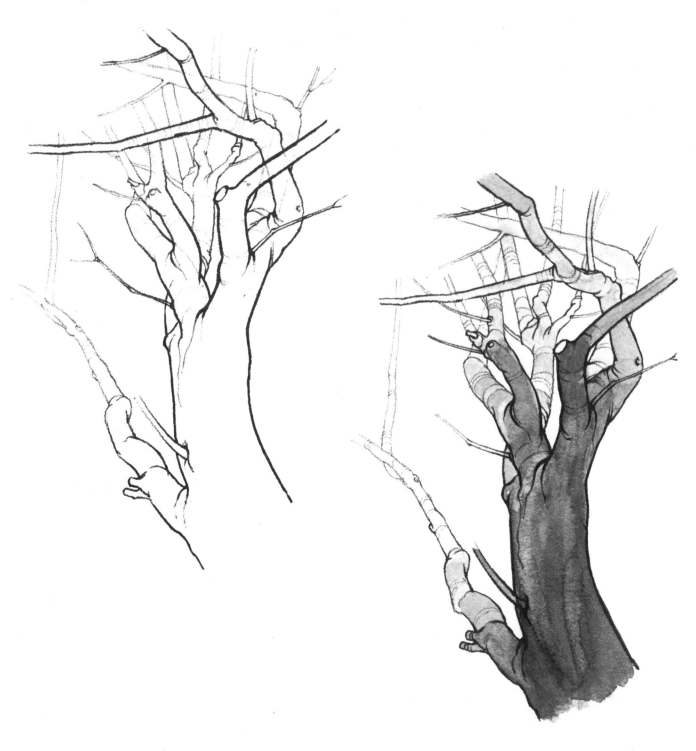